BUILD YOUR BRAND
THE 10 ESSENTIAL STEPS BEFORE LAUNCHING YOUR BUSINESS

By Daniela Torres

ISBN 978-0-9951912-2-8
ISBN-10 0995191220

ABOUT ME

My name is Daniela Torres. I'm originally a journalist, with a Bachelor Degree in Communications and a Post Graduate degree in Marketing, Business Management and People Management.

As a journalist I've worked in different fields and was always involved in everything that was connected to media and communications. I worked in a news website, then I spent a few years in magazines, where I eventually became an editor in chief. I left the news and became a professor in a university, where I taught Photography, Marketing Writing and Graphic Design. Then I moved to corporate, worked at IBM for a couple years, which was very good for my career.

Then I put all of my knowledge and experience together and started working for my first client as a Press Officer/PR/Personal Branding. That was back in 2010, which is when I realized I was so passionate about being part of every step of creating a brand. The concept, the graphic design, the marketing, social media, all of it. I started taking other clients and officially opened what I initially called a marketing company and became more and more involved in how the branding process works. I got the best partner ever, my husband Rod. It is pretty hard to work with your life partner but I can't imagine myself not working with him, he's so good! Together we created KIAI Agency, which is a branding agency based in Vancouver, Canada. We specialized in creating brands and making them a success. Now I'm here to teach you how to build your brand in 10 essential steps. I hope you like it!

CONTENTS

INTRODUCTION

What is this book about? Why do I need a brand? How and when should I start? I will try to answer all of these questions and hopefully much more. But let's begin with some of the terms you will see on this book:

BRAND
By definition (and according to Google) the word Brand means: *1. a type of product manufactured by a particular company under a particular name. (Ex: "a new brand of detergent")*
synonyms: make, line, label, marque;   2. an identifying mark burned on livestock or (especially formerly) criminals or slaves with a branding iron.
synonyms: identification, marker, earmark. (Ex: "the brand on a sheep")

When we talk about Brand in this book, we are referring to definition number 1, and the purpose of this book is to exactly build this identity, this essence that belongs to a company, a business, a startup, etc.

BRANDING
It's very common for people to think that Branding is the same as logo or Visual Identity. It's not, at all. Branding is a strategy that defines the experience that a customer or client will have with a certain brand. And I mean the experience in every single step. Not only in sales or customer service. It starts with the brand's purpose and its culture and it reflects in the marketing and all the ways that the brand will be in contact with its consumers.

With that being said, what does it mean to create a brand after all?

When you finish this book, you will know exactly what your brand is. You will be able to explain it for an investor, for a business partner, for your bank, for your employees (if you have them), for your supporters and, mostly, for those who are going to buy your product or service.

Most people know what is their brand or their business but they have a hard time explaining or presenting it to other people. That happens when there are gaps in the definition of your brand. You kind of know who your target audience is, but you don't know how to reach them. Maybe you know that you're different, but you don't know how to differentiate yourself from your competitors. Over the next 10 steps, we'll work to fill up all of those possible gaps and you'll be able to understand your brand and tell people about it in a simple effective way.

How does this book work?

This book was created using the same method I use with my clients, except that I send them questionnaires in Word or Pages files in which they can write on the computer and send me the answers or they can print it and handwrite the answers. So you have to either copy/print the book or write down the questions and answers. What matters is that this book is an easy, practical and effective guideline for you and the way you will be guided will be by answering the questions. This method is highly effective because it is the best way for you to create real content, written by you and for you. By the end of this book, the material you will have will be unique and you will own it.

Who should be reading this book?

Well, you would love to hire someone to create your brand and do all the marketing for you, but you can't afford it. So you are willing to do everything you can to make your business work but you need some guidance, you need a hand. You know who you are and what you want with your business but you need to organize everything in a way that it's easy, practical, fast and works. You have a great idea but you just don't know what to do with it. Or maybe you have already started but you feel like there's something missing. If you see yourself somewhere in the above description, we got your back. Enjoy this. I would've loved to been able to access this book when I started my own business. Let's get started.

STEP 1: THE 5W2H

I have no idea who invented it but this technique is really useful. The 5W2H is a tool that will force you to go deeper in your thoughts and ideas when you are building your brand's foundation. It stands for the 7 questions: What, Why, Who, When, Where, How and How Much - I think it's supposed to be How Many but I've been using it as How Much.

I want you to relax, go to a quiet place where you can be in peace, grab a notebook or some paper and answer these questions as if you were explaining things for a 12-year-old.

See, you're not supposed to write this for yourself. You already know how this works. You're sold. The little girl, let's call her Amber, she has no idea who you are and what is your business about. You might think that your business has nothing to do with Amber, but Amber is really smart and if she can't understand your business or even be interested about it, nobody else will.

So please, explain to Amber, plain and simple:

1.1) WHAT is your business, service or product? (Explain it with as much detail possible)
Answer:

_____

_____

_____

_____

_____

_____

_____

_____

_____

_____

_____
_____
_____
_____
_____
_____
_____
_____
_____
_____
_____

When you're done, read it out loud.

Great! Now, I want you to explain it again. This time, summarize your text so that it is 40% shorter than your first answer.

What is your business, service or product?
Answer:

_____
_____
_____
_____
_____
_____
_____
_____
_____
_____
_____

Great. Let's save this for later.

1.2) WHY your business, service or product was created? Why for you, why for them, why for the whole world. Why do this and not something else?

Answer:

_____
_____
_____
_____
_____
_____
_____
_____
_____
_____
_____
_____
_____
_____

1.3) WHO is it made for? All the target audiences you can think of and how would they use it.

Answer:

_____
_____
_____
_____
_____
_____
_____
_____
_____
_____
_____
_____
_____
_____

_____

_____

_____

_____

_____

_____

_____

_____

_____

_____

Let's get to the bottom of it. Establishing your target audience.

Choose the options that match your target audience and write down below the result of your options. Ex: I own a dancing studio specific for teenage girls from Seattle who like to dance. Note: This is a guideline that might not literally fit you. You could have an online business with products for everybody to buy. In this case your target audience could be people from all over the world that want to buy [whatever] for them to use for their [whatever].

There is always a target audience and people usually think that the wider the better, but it's the very opposite. You have to find your niche and then communicate with them. Do things for them and not for a general audience.

For B2C (Business to Consumers/People)
1.3.1) [Gender] Boys   Girls   Men   Women   People
   Other
1.3.2) [Age] Infant   Toddler   Child   Teenager   Young Adult
   Adults   Nature   Seniors   Other
1.3.3) [From] Neighborhood City   Country   Other Not
Applicable
1.3.4) Who [verb/action/their need/what you will provide]

Your target audience is:

_____

_____

_____

_____

_____

_____

Now complete the sentence: I own a ...

_____

_____

_____

_____

_____

_____

For B2B (Business for Business)
1.3.5) [What] Business Organization Charity Other
1.3.6) [From] Neighborhood City Country Other Not
Applicable
1.3.7) Who [verb/action/their need/what you will provide]
Your target audience is:

_____

_____

_____

_____

_____

Now complete the sentence: I own a ...

_____

_____

_____

_____

_____

_____

1.4) WHEN these people should use your product/service? At what point you become a better or perfect solution for them?
Answer:

_____
_____
_____
_____
_____
_____
_____
_____
_____
_____
_____
_____
_____
_____
_____

1.5) WHERE your business, service or product is being, will be or should be promoted?
Answer:

_____
_____
_____
_____
_____
_____
_____
_____
_____
_____
_____
_____
_____
_____

1.6) HOW your business, service or product will change the way things are done right now?
Answer:

_____

_____

_____

_____

_____

_____

_____

_____

_____

_____

_____

_____

_____

_____

_____

_____

1.7) HOW MUCH will your business, service or product cost?
Remember, Amber wants to know all the details.
Answer:

_____

_____

_____

_____

_____

_____

_____

_____

_____

_____

_____

_____

_____

_____

_____

Are you with me? You might be either loving this, or you're overwhelmed, bored, thinking this is too hard or not understanding where this is going to go, but trust me, all of this will make sense and will be totally worth it.

STEP 2: RESEARCH

It doesn't matter how big your business is or will be, you always have to pay attention to the market, the trends and the competition. Here are some questions that you should ask yourself when creating your brand:

Does the market need what I'm offering? Does the market want what I'm offering? Is the market saturated? Have I checked demographic and/or economic trends in my industry?

As a business owner, you have to pay close attention to identify opportunities and red flags. If you got to the point that you are creating your brand, we are assuming you already made a big research on the topics we wrote above. The research we are talking about below is in order to understand where your competitors stand and where you stand in the market.

2.1 Write down the name (and business) of at least 3 competitors.
Note: Some businesses are very innovative and they might not have a direct competitor but every business in the world have a direct and indirect competition. An indirect competition is the one that sells not exactly your product or service but could satisfy your customer's need. The direct competitor is the one that sells essentially the same thing you do. Try to be as close to direct as possible.
Answer:

_____

_____

_____

_____

_____

_____

_____

_____

_____

_____
_____
_____
_____
_____
_____
_____
_____
_____
_____
_____
_____
_____
_____
_____
_____
_____
_____

2.2 Write down five reasons why your business, service or product is better than certain competitors.

Answer:

_____
_____
_____
_____
_____
_____
_____
_____
_____
_____
_____
_____
_____
_____
_____

_____
_____
_____
_____
_____
_____
_____
_____
_____
_____

2.3 Write down five reasons why your business, service or product is worse than certain competitors.
Answer:

_____
_____
_____
_____
_____
_____
_____
_____
_____
_____
_____
_____
_____
_____
_____
_____
_____
_____
_____
_____

Good job. Remember: A good marketing strategy should showcase your 5 top qualities while you work hard to overcome your 5 weaknesses.

STEP 3: POSITION

Now that you wrote down where you stand and where the competition stands, let's work on your positioning.

The Brand Positioning describes how a brand is different from its competitors. Every brand needs to differentiate itself in a way.

If you are starting right now you probably think your competitors are way ahead of you (and they probably are) but they are also making (or have made) many mistakes. You have the advantage of looking at all of them and say "None of them is doing this or that". Sometimes differentiation is a big thing, sometimes it's a little detail. You can have a different approach like "We'll be cooler, we'll be cheaper, we'll be faster, we'll be slower, we'll be more friendly" etc. It could be a visual aspect like "we'll be prettier, we'll be fancier, we'll be simpler, we'll be more colorful". It could also be a high investment difference, like "we'll have more structure, we'll be bigger, we'll have a better technology" or just a style like "we'll be classic, modern, geeky, funny". The thing is: You have to stand out some how (or many hows).

If you're thinking about joining the market by being just another one, stop right now! It's not necessarily about being better, it's how you are different from the others. People are different, so what is good for someone might not be interesting for another.

How do you work in your Brand Positioning, then? You have to understand that the **positioning is the perfect junction between the attraction (what customers want) and the distinction (what only you can give).**

3.1 What does your business, service or product offer that is interesting for its target audience?

Answer:

_____

_____

_____

_____

_____

_____

_____

_____

_____

_____

_____

_____

_____

_____

_____

_____

_____

3.2 What does your business, service or product offer that is special for its target audience?

Answer:

_____

_____

_____

_____

_____

_____

_____

_____

_____

_____

_____

_____

_____

_____

_____

3.3 In what ways and/or how can your customers experience this (that you just wrote) once they buy your service or product?
Answer:

_____
_____
_____
_____
_____
_____
_____
_____
_____
_____
_____
_____
_____

3.4 Now put the three answers together and create a short statement. For example: "(3.1) We at [your business] make/offer whatever product or service for [target audience], (3.2) but we specialized in [your differentiation] so our clients can experience (3.3)".
Answer:

_____
_____
_____
_____
_____
_____
_____
_____
_____
_____
_____
_____
_____

Continue only when you are satisfied with this answers, because they will be extremely important for your business. I'm serious, you can't continue without finishing this. Don't rush yourself. This is the right time and maybe the only time you have to do this.

STEP 4: PROMISE

This is very exciting. Your brand is being shaped and now it's time for you to create a commitment with your clients, customers, employees, business partners, suppliers and anybody that could possibly be involved with your brand.

The Brand Promise is the commitment that your business will have to keep at all times - not only for advertising purposes. This will be the summary of your soul, the description your DNA.

Your brand promise is what will create loyal customers.

Who doesn't want to be involved with someone that keeps their word? Brands that consistently keep their promises can become very powerful, so keeping this promise is a must.

The Brand Promise needs to follow 3 rules: 1) It must be unique; 2) It must be believable and 3) (again) It must be kept at all times.

Here are some examples of brand promises:

FedEx – Your package will get there overnight. Guaranteed.
IKEA – To provide well-designed quality products at an affordable price.
Disney – Where dreams come true.

Sometimes the promise becomes their tagline, like:
Walmart: Save Money, Live Better
Panasonic: Ideas for Life

Sometimes it's not a statement or a tagline, but just a concept, like
Volvo: Safe cars

4.1 What are the things that your customers will always have? Write down as many things you like.
Answer:

_____
_____
_____
_____
_____
_____
_____
_____
_____
_____
_____
_____
_____
_____
_____
_____
_____
_____
_____

4.2 Now let's build a statement: What is your business, service or product's official promise?
Answer:

_____
_____
_____
_____
_____
_____
_____
_____
_____

Is this promise unique? Is it believable? Is it possible to keep at all times? If you answered YES to those 3 questions you can move on to step 5.

STEP 5: MISSION, VISION AND VALUES

What is the difference between a Brand Promise and a mission statement? They can look like they are the same, but they're not. While the Brand Promise is the commitment that your business makes with its employees, partners and clients, the mission statement is the description of what your business do, from an internal perspective. According to Peter Drucker, "the effective mission statement is short and sharply focused. It should fit on a T-shirt. The mission says why you do what you do, not the means by which you do it".

And why should you have mission, vision and values statements? So you can create your business's culture, as well as attract and engage the right people for your team. If you don't have a team right now, create those statements for yourself. If you are your own team you have to establish this right now and always follow your mission, vision and values as your guidelines.

5.1 Creating your mission statement.

Here are some examples to get you inspired:
Google - To organize the world's information and make it universally accessible and useful.

AT&T - To connect people with their world, everywhere they live and work, and do it better than anyone else.

Amazon - To be Earth's most customer-centric company where people can find and discover anything they want to buy online.

(A not so big company) Rendezvous Hair Salon - We want to make your salon experience as unique and memorable as you are.

As you can see, it's common to use an action, to whom and sometimes where. Now, remember items 1.1, 1.2 and 1.3? Use them to answer the 3 questions below:

5.1.1) Why does the company exist?
A:

_____

_____

_____

_____

_____

_____

_____

_____

_____

_____

_____

_____

_____

_____

_____

_____

_____

5.1.2) What does the company do?
A:

_____

_____

_____

_____

_____

_____

_____

_____

_____

_____

5.1.3) For who?
A:

_____
_____
_____
_____
_____
_____
_____
_____
_____
_____
_____
_____

5.1.4) Your mission is:
A:

_____
_____
_____
_____
_____
_____
_____
_____

5.2 Creating your vision statement.
When defining the vision of a business, you have to established the outlook for long-term. The vision is inspired by what you aim for the future, as long as it's an attainable, realistic dream. It should contain both the aspiration and inspiration, and reflect the aim being sought by individual efforts, by the efforts of your team and by the investment you're willing to make. Here are some examples to get you inspired:

Starbucks - To establish Starbucks as the most recognized and respected brand in the world.

Avon - To be the company that best understands and satisfies the product, service and self-fulfillment needs of women - globally.

Heinz - To be the world's premier food company, offering nutritious, superior tasting foods to people everywhere.

(A not so big company) Mill City Farmers Market - To be a nationally recognized marketplace model that connects, educates and empowers a community to support a healthy, sustainable food system to contribute to the success of local food growers and producers.

As you can see, there is a verb that is a goal, then the details of this goal and to whom. Answer the 3 questions below:

5.2.1) What is your long-term goal? / What would you like to accomplish?
A:

_____

_____

_____

_____

_____

_____

_____

_____

5.2.2) How can your business make an impact in a [community, city, state/province, country, etc.]? Item 1.6 will help you with that.
A:

_____

_____

_____

_____
_____
_____
_____
_____
_____
_____
_____
_____
_____
_____
_____

5.2.3) Your vision is:
A:

_____
_____
_____
_____
_____
_____
_____
_____
_____

5.3 Defining your values

Values are the principles or beliefs of your business. They work as a guideline for the behaviors, attitudes and decisions of every person that is evolved with your company, product or service. Meaning, the values must be present in the daily lives of employees and the company's relationships with customers, suppliers and partners. Here are some examples to get you inspired:

Coca-Cola - Leadership: The courage to shape a better future; Collaboration: Leverage collective genius; Integrity: Be real; Accountability: If it is to be, it's up to me; Passion: Committed in heart and mind; Diversity: As inclusive as our brands; Quality: What we do, we do well

IBM - Dedication to every client's success; Innovation that matters - for our company and for the world; Trust and personal responsibility in all relationships.

Mercedes-Benz - The audacity to reject compromise; The instinct to protect what matters; The commitment to honor a legacy; The vision to consider every detail; The foresight to take responsibility; The ingenuity to outperform expectations.

You can also use only the words, like
Barnes & Noble Booksellers - Customer Service, Quality, Empathy, Respect, Integrity, Responsibility, Teamwork

5.3.1) What are the core values of your business, service or product:
A:

_____
_____
_____
_____
_____
_____
_____
_____
_____
_____
_____

You are done with your brand's concept! Great job!

STEP 6: THE LOGO & BRAND ID

Congratulations, your brand has a soul and now we will create a face for it, meaning: a logo!

You will find below some great tips to create the perfect logo but before you move forward, I have to be honest with you. If a new business can't afford to invest in a logo, it probably shouldn't be opening at this point. A bad logo can make the company or product look amateurish, cheap, unskilled and unreliable. Certainly not the best way to start, right?

There is scientific proof that graphic design can change the way customers behave. Images can either attract or repel people. A good logo and visual identity can actually motivate your customers to buy from you, by triggering emotions. Thankfully, you can hire professionals to make sure your brand looks the best it can.

Here are 7 steps to ensure you will create the perfect logo:

6.1) Hire a professional
When you start a business, there are so many things to take into consideration and a lot of expenses. Unfortunately, some people try to "save money" by choosing not to hire a professional to design a brand identity until the first clients come along or (sometimes even worse) they create the logo themselves, possibly with the help of an inexperienced friend.
Not investing in your logo is one of the worst things you can do for your new business as this action can result in your business failure.

6.2) Make sure the concept is well defined
Remember your What, Your Positioning, Your Promise, Your Statements? Now that you thought about all of that, there are some exercises to understand what is the face to this brand. You can deliver the answers below to a graphic designer. He/She will be very thankful for your direction.

6.2.1 How would you describe your business, service or product if it was a person entering in the room?
Answer:

_____
_____
_____
_____
_____
_____
_____

6.2.2. In what ways physically your business, service or product would call people's attention?
Answer:

_____
_____
_____
_____
_____
_____
_____

6.2.3 In what ways your business, service or product would call people's attention in terms of personality?
Answer:

_____
_____
_____
_____
_____
_____
_____

6.2.4 Would you say your logo is:

a. masculine or feminine? A:

b. young or mature? A:

c. luxurious or economic? A:

d. modern or classic? A:

e. playful or serious? A:

f. noisy or quiet? A:

g. simple or complex? A:

h. subtle and mysterious or obvious and direct? A:

6.2.5 What colors would you like to use?

Yellow: Optimism, Clarity and Warmth. Commonly used by the automotive and food industries.

Orange: Friendly, Cheerful, Confidence. Commonly used for food, art and sports.

Red: Excitement, Youthful, Bold. Commonly used for food, business and entertainment logos.

Purple: Creative, Luxury, Wise. Commonly used for Beauty & Health, chocolate and spiritual themes.

Pink: Feminism, Innocence, Youth and Beauty. Commonly used for beauty, fashion and toys.

Blue: Trust, Strength, Loyalty. Commonly used for software, finance, pharmaceutical industry, government and banks.

Green: Peaceful, Growth, Health. Commonly used for healthy food products, agriculture, recycling and other environmentally friendly companies.

White: Balance, Neutral, Calm. Found in logos as reversed text or negative space.

Black: Elegant, Authority, Power. Commonly used to target youth and a high-end audience.

The color(s) I will use is/are:

_____

_____

_____

_____

6.2.6 What kind of logotype would you like?

a. WORD MARK - Your company name in a stylized type font becomes the logo
Ex: Coca-Cola

b. PICTORIAL MARK - an image or shape that is easily recognizable is used to represent your company /business
Ex: The M from McDonald's

c. ABSTRACT MARK - an abstract shape or symbol is used to convey the values of your business
Ex: Olympic Games (circles) symbol

d. LETTER FORM – letters/initials from your business name are used to create a logo
Ex: IBM

e. EMBLEM – business name enveloped by a pictorial element or shape
Ex: Ford

f. CHARACTER – a character or mascot to represent your business
Ex: Lacoste

A: My logo will be a:

_____

6.3) Balance, size and functionality
It is important that the logo is balanced, keeping the 'weight' of graphics, colors and symmetry. There are techniques to ensure that.

Size is also a strategic point because the logo should be visually pleasing and readable in multiple dimensions.

Functionality is also essential. The logo should work in high-resolution and low-resolution, both horizontally and vertically, with or without a box around it, printed, screened, embroidered on a shirt... Possibilities are endless, so versatility is key.

6.4) The choice of color

The ideal is to use palettes that match the field of business, avoiding bright and dazzling colors. Understanding the colors and their effect on people are also an asset. It's definitely possible to influence a customer with the right combination.

Regardless of the palette choice, the logo has to be adaptable to black and white, grayscale and two colors.

6.5) A current style

The market is constantly changing. Maybe there's a trend in the industry or in design?

You want to stand out but not by being so different that people can't understand what or who you are. The logo can not look obsolete. In fact, it needs to look timeless, even though at one point it will have adjustments, maybe every decade, which is perfectly normal.

6.6) Typography

This is also related to style as some areas are more limited in the typography and don't allow too much adventure.

As much as possible, designer and contractor should try font options such as serif, sans serif, bold, script, italic or customized. Of course, the designer should only present the options that fit well with the figure. Whatever you choose, just make sure your text is readable in big and small sizes.

6.7) Recognition

A successful logo is one that is easily recognized by the public. It means that it's memorable, which is a big deal in a market full of competitors.

Also, the more it gets recognized the bigger is the emotional bond created between the brand and the customer. This link strengthens customer loyalty.
Voilà! These are the 7 steps to create a perfect logo. Once you have that, you should move to the next step.

6.8 Your BRAND ID

So, now that you have the concept of your brand and your logo, what are the graphic design materials you should have?

For a business that is starting, it is recommended to a least make a stationery, which will make you look more professional for your customers. Stationery is, generally, all the graphic designs that show your brand on paper, such as business cards and letterhead. Even if your business is mostly or only online, you have to create some stationery, like a digital signature and a personalized invoice. Everything that you can create in terms of stationery will make you look more professional. In certain occasions, not having a business card can make you look like an unreliable person. Here are some basic examples of nice stationery materials:

Business card
Letterhead
Invoice
Envelope
Corporate Folder

You can also create promo gifts like pens or pencils. This is a good way to promote your business because you're giving someone something that it's useful and has your name on it. There are many websites that have all kinds of promo gifts available for small or big orders. Here are some basic examples of nice promo gifts:

Pens
Pencils
USB Drive
Water Bottle
Coffee Mug
Eco Bag
T-Shirts
Hats
Notebooks

STEP 7: THE GRAPHICS

Besides stationary and promo gifts, one of the most important things you have to think about is your marketing/sales/advertising material. Before you launch, make sure you already have some pamphlets or a banner for an online business.

You would be surprised on how powerful pamphlets can be. If you want to start (or already have) a B2C business that sells either a product or service, try printing 500 hundred pamphlets or coupons and distribute them around your neighborhood so people can know you exist. There are some places (like condos) that you are not allowed to distribute junk mail. If you are not sure on how to proceed, you can always hire a delivering service to make sure your target audience gets your material.

Anyway, make sure you take some time to think how you are going to present yourself for your customers or clients. Here are some basic examples of nice sales materials:

Catalogs
Brochures
Media Kits
Banners
Newsletter template

Of everything you just read, if your budget is really tight in a way that is impossible for you to do the basic, make sure you have at least a business card and a professionally made pamphlet - printed and/or online. You can not start a business without these two items.

STEP 8: THE ONLINE PRESENCE

What will your customers see when they find you on Google? I think that if you are reading this book I don't need to tell you in details how much is going on in the internet in terms of business transactions. Did you know that every 30 seconds, online retail sales reach US$1 million? Every 30 seconds! That's just one number for eCommerce.

All the connections that are involved on the web, everything that it represents all over the world makes it impossible to understand how a business owner thinks they don't have to be online. Even if you own a tiny shop that is only for your neighbors, you can use the web to connect with people. How do you think most people find out about places these days? Walking around? No! They go online to find local businesses, and they even get to see customer's opinions and recommendations. That's just how it works. So if you're not there, trust me, somebody else will be.

A competitor can literally steal your clients using the internet. They can do it by talking to them on social media and promoting a sale; or they can send an email with a coupon; or they can create this amazing blog that will share so much information that no matter how much you know how things work in your field, it just won't look like you know as much as your sympathetic teacher competitor does. There's no escape, really. Plus, being on the internet is so much fun!

Your online presence should be built based on a strategy that you will have to create yourself - unless you have the funds to hire someone, but if you're reading this, you probably want to do this yourself, except for the logo. Please tell me you hired someone to do your logo? Ok, moving on.

To build your online presence strategy you have to create a plan by asking yourself the following questions:

8.1 What are my goals on the internet?

This will create a path, like, if you want to sell your product online, you have to create an eCommerce website. If you have a lot of information to share, you have to create a blog. If you just want to be there and you're not sure yet, just create a simple website.

So the first thing you have to decide is if you're going to create:
a) a website;
b) a blog;
c) an Ecommerce;
d) all three;
e) a Facebook page. Yes, there are some businesses that start creating only a Facebook page. It can be done, because you probably know how to use it and you can post things yourself, you can engage, you can promote whatever you need. It is possible to start slow with a Facebook page, IF your target audience is there. Most people are on Facebook, but only you can tell if your target audience is there. And you can use Facebook advertising tools to reach your exact target audience. It's very intuitive and can give you great results to start.

Don't think you don't need a website. Your website is your online business card. Remember what I said before about how not having a business card can make you look unprofessional and possibly unreliable? So, once you have the funds or know exactly what do you want with your website, you must create it. You can hire someone (please, do), or use some great user friendly platforms like Wix (the simplest one in my opinion), Webflow and SquareSpace.

8.2 Social Media

If you own a business, you have to be social. 74% of the customers are influenced by social media when purchasing their product. Let's put it this way: If your website is like your online business card, your social media is like your online customer service, your showcase, your advertising channel, your voice, your style, all together. You just have-to-be-there. I know I already said that, I just want to make sure you understand.

The first thing you have to do is (surprisingly) not a Facebook Page, but a Google+ Business Page. You can Google how to create one - it's very simple - I just want to give you the reasons why you must have a Google+ for your business. Do you know how you put a name of a business on Google Search and it shows you the name, the address (connected to Google Maps), the phone and a website of this business? This is provided by the Google+ page and nothing else. As if you would need another reason to create your Google+ page, know that everything you post on G+ is immediately indexed by Google. Which means that the more you post there, the more you will be found by Google when people look for you or for something similar that will make new customers find you.

All the other social media options should be chosen according to your commitment. You don't have to be everywhere. In fact, you have to be consistent where you can be, in terms of investing time to provide content or the time to search for good content, whatever is applicable for your business.

Facebook is by far the most used social media in the world. There's also Twitter which is very popular and is getting more and more visual, and you can keep it simple by posting your message in only 140 characters. However, a good Twitter account is one that it's always interacting with other Twitter users by liking other tweets, retweeting and so on.

If you think a picture is worth a thousand words, you're absolutely right and if you have a good camera in your smartphone and a good taste for pictures, you should invest on Instagram. Also, Pinterest is a great tool to promote your business. Their internal search engine is really good, it's like their private Google and it works perfectly, for free.

Depending on your line of business, specially if you are a B2B, you should probably be on LinkedIn. It's a networking social media. So you can use it to attract business clients, generate leads and even use it as a recruiting tool.

Now, if you want to invest on the most growing platform in the world, make sure you produce videos for YouTube, Vimeo, Snapchat and everything that end up being released in the market. There are serious researches that estimate that, by 2020, 70% of the internet content will be on video. If it's going to be 70% or not, for sure it's something to think about. You can do videos of your products, service, personal profile, animations, commercials, create an expert channel... the possibilities are endless.

STEP 9: THE SALES

We have reached a point where you have: 1) your Brand Strategy, 2) your logo, 3) your graphic design materials, 4) your website and 5) your social media ready to go. Having all of this will certainly make a great impact in the market, but there's something I want to make sure you nailed before launching your business: Your sales strategy.

There's a tool in Marketing called "The 4 P's": Product, Place, Price and Promotion. This system was created back on the 1960's and is absolutely necessary to the present day. Here's how it works. You have to make sure you have covered all 4 P's. Once you do, your sales and marketing strategy will be ready - or at least will have a great start.

9.1 The Product: What is it that you're selling?
We already have this statement ready, in item 3.4 of this book.
A:

_____
_____
_____
_____
_____
_____
_____
_____
_____
_____
_____

Anything else you want to add?

_____
_____
_____

9.2 The Place: Where your business, service or product can be found?

Will you have your own store? Will you sell it online and offline? Will you work with third parties and/or business partners? Will you work with intensive distribution, exclusive distribution, selective distribution, franchising?

You need to have this information organized before launching your business, so then your new customers can know where to find you immediately. Once they do go after you, you're effectively there.
A:

_____
_____
_____
_____
_____
_____
_____
_____
_____
_____
_____
_____
_____
_____
_____
_____
_____
_____
_____
_____
_____
_____
_____
_____

9.3 The Price: How much does your business, service or product cost?

You already answered that in item 1.7, just make sure is accurate and ready to be available for your new clients in your website and your sales material, online, offline, etc.

A:

_____
_____
_____
_____
_____
_____
_____
_____
_____
_____
_____
_____
_____
_____
_____
_____
_____
_____
_____
_____
_____
_____
_____
_____
_____
_____
_____
_____

9.4 The Promotion: The strategy to promote your business.

Online and offline advertising? Sales promotion, social media marketing, email marketing, search engine marketing?

9.4.1 What are the best channels to reach your clients? Online and offline.
A:

_____
_____
_____
_____
_____
_____
_____

9.4.2 When is the best time to start promoting your business?
A:

_____
_____
_____
_____
_____
_____
_____

9.4.3 How much budget do you have available?
A:

_____
_____
_____
_____
_____
_____
_____

9.4.5 So what will be your official strategy to promote your business?

A:

_____

_____

_____

_____

_____

_____

_____

_____

_____

_____

_____

_____

_____

The promotion is crucial, because if you are building this amazing brand, you have to make sure people will be able to see it, find it and tell other people about it.

STEP 10: THE LAUNCH

Or relaunch, because if you already own a business but took all the 9 steps before, you're about to relaunch it. How exciting is that?

Your brand is ready for the world. What a crazy ride so far. All you want to do is to start, and you will. But the step is divided in 2 separate phases. An organized launch must be made from top to bottom and from the inside out. Meaning: upper management first, then employees and everybody involved, then your final customer/client.

Phase 1: Internal Launch
For who? All your employees, business partners, investors, suppliers, vendors or whoever is evolved with your brand that is not a client or customer.

These people will have a chance to deeply understand what is your brand promise, your positioning, your target audience. Everything that you created in the 8 steps below. Not only they will become an ambassador of your brand but sharing this information will create a good relationship inside your business and you will even be able to get some feedback before going public.

Phase 2: External Launch
For who? The second launch is for the public, aka your customers or clients.

Depending on your budget you can do a party, a cocktail, a sale… Whatever you decide, just make sure there is an official "Grand Opening", even if it's only online. Make sure you share the information with the world.

A few things to consider in your launch.

10.1 Choose the perfect timing.
10.2 Make sure your 4P's strategy is totally ready
10.3 Unveil your brand by not only showing your logo and graphic design, but specially by presenting them your brand promise.
10.4 Make sure you get feedback from your clients or customers. Stimulate them to talk to you, show the you care.

A FINAL TOUCH

Congratulations on concluding this book! This is it. If you followed the steps, you are ready. I am so proud of you, I hope you are too!

If you want to make your own brand's bible, you can write up a report with:
Your Brand Statement (Item 1.1)
Your Brand Promise (Item 4.2)
Your Mission, Vision and Values (Step 5)
The 4P's (Items 9.1-9.4)

This way you can make sure that you have easy access to the main content of your Branding Strategy.

All the best,
Daniela Torres

PS: I'd love to know how do you feel after your Branding is done. Feel free to write your review at the book's sales page. This helps me a lot. ☺

BUILD YOUR BRAND
THE 10 ESSENTIAL STEPS BEFORE LAUNCHING YOUR BUSINESS

By Daniela Torres

ISBN 978-0-9951912-2-8
ISBN-10 0995191220

www.ingramcontent.com/pod-product-compliance
Lightning Source LLC
Chambersburg PA
CBHW071610200326
41519CB00021BB/6946

YOUR

BRILLIANT

CAREER GOALS

A 6 step plan to find out what you
REALLY want to do – whether you
want to do something completely
different, have reached a career
crossroads, or want to check you
are going in the right direction

ANNASHEATHER